# Ruby Programming For Beginners

## The Simple Guide to Learning Ruby Programming Language Fast!

# Table Of Contents

# Introduction

I want to thank you and congratulate you for downloading the book Ruby Programming for Beginners.

This book contains proven steps and strategies on how to become a truly skilled Ruby programmer.

This book will explain the basics of Ruby, right up to some advanced sections of code. You will learn the different uses or Ruby, and why it's an important still to have as a programmer.

You will soon discover how to write code in Ruby, and begin performing simple functions!

If you do not develop your skill right off the bat, do not get discouraged. Programming takes practice and time, but this is a great place to begin!

It's time for you to become an amazing programmer, now get typing!

# Chapter 1: What is Ruby Programming and what is it used for?

In this chapter you are going to learn what Ruby Programming is and what it is used for. So, strap in and put on your thinking cap, you are about to dive into a new world where programming is essential. This book will dive into this programming language and will assume that you do not even have experience with HTML. So, you are in safe hands. Ruby is a specific language that is object oriented. It has unique and special characteristics and quirks that will be explained later on in the book.

## What is Ruby Programming?

Ruby as said, is a language that is object oriented. It was built to be more user friendly. It is easy enough to learn and perform, while it is still powerful enough to offer experienced programmers the tools they need. Yukihiro Matsumoto is the architect of this new, high in demand language.

## What is it used for?

Ruby is normally used for script language applications like text processing or even middleware programs. It is suitable for ad-hoc tasks that were normally solved with Perl. Writing simple programs using Ruby is extremely easy. It is almost like a sequence of events type of programming.

This language is also great for larger types of software systems; for example, Ruby on Rails. Ruby on Rails has five main subsystems, a lot of minor pieces, a large bank of support scripts, libraries, and database back-ends.

# Three Reason Why Ruby Should be Learned

There are three serious reasons why you should take Ruby seriously. It can advance you professionally and also give you an outlet to creativity, it could maybe even help you to start up your own company with a game that you create.

### Reason #1: It is one of the easiest languages to learn.

Ruby is said to be a higher level of programming language, even higher than C++. It has strong abstractions from computer details. It offers easier learning than other program languages.

### Reason #2: It is a stepping-stone to using Ruby on Rails.

If you are a bit familiar with the programming world, you have probably heard of Ruby on Rails. Rails is a framework software that will enable you to create web applications. There are students that are new to programming that are not sure what the difference is between the two. Ruby is the language, whereas Ruby on Rails is the framework that depends on the Ruby language. Rails is almost like a template of already written codes.

### Reason #3: Those with Ruby skills are in very high demand.

Ruby is listed in the TIOBE Programming Community Index at number thirteen for the most sought after programming language. It is high in demand and growing beyond belief..

# Chapter 2: Evaluation by Your Computer for Ruby Codes

The main brain of the language called the interpreter, reads your code from the top to the bottom, and then from the left to the right. It goes from line one, character one and then first reads across line one to the last character. It then will go down to the next line, and so on until it is done with the last line of the code.

If you have an error in your code, called a syntax error, then it will stop and show you where you messed up. It will respond with the line number that corresponds to the error in the code. This is important to remember when you begin as you will encounter errors while you are coding. You will need to understand how to decipher the errors. At times, this is not straightforward when you are a beginner.

This is top-down parsing. It can also affect the control of the flow of the logic in the program. If you want to calculate a balance of an individual's account before you show them, then you would have to ensure that a method, as well as a function is included that does the calculation before the output. This means that if you are outputting a balance on line 10, then it will have to do the calculations somewhere from line 1 to 9. I know this may seem a little confusing right now, but you will get it as we move along.

# Chapter 3: What are Ruby Objects and Methods?

In this chapter you will learn about Ruby Objects and Ruby Methods. This will help you begin to understand the program. You will learn how to interpret objects and learn a few methods.

## Ruby Objects

Of course when thinking of the term "object" you think of an item or thing. This is true in programming as well. This goes back to the previous statement of Ruby being an object oriented programming language. That means that it manipulates the data in the assumption that the data in question is an object. There are other languages that are also object oriented, but there are few that put the object in the center of the focus like Ruby does.

In Ruby, everything is considered an object. It means that every variable and every operation is or deals with an object. Just like physical objects, in Ruby each object has different characteristics. A string is considered an object and has characteristics built in that will make it suitable for the handling text.

## Ruby Methods

Just like the typical definition of method, the meaning in programming language is the same, it is a definition of a certain action. The object performs this action. Ruby includes a built in library of object methods and definitions.

One method is "capitalize" for Ruby class "strings". We will cover strings in another section of this book.

```
1    string1 = "this string is awesome"
```

If you wrote string1.capitalize, the output would look something like this:

```
     "This string is awesome"
1
```

The capitalize method tells the Ruby interpreter to convert the first character of this string to go from lowercase to uppercase. Another thing that you may have noticed is the way to name a method. This code: String1.captialize is basically {{object name}} . {{method name}} . In this case, the specific object is the string variable. If you were to try and "capitalize" on an object that includes no string, it would throw up an error. You are able to create any method for the objects. Here is the way to do it:

```
1    def method_name

2       #Enter code here

3    end
```

The number sign (#) is to tell the interpreter that this is a comment meant for a human and it should ignore it. The interpreter will ignore this line and skip it.

# Chapter 4: What are Ruby Classes and Instances?

A Ruby class is a blueprint. It will allow you to create different objects of different types, and allows you to create methods in relation to those objects. However, classes have a special property. This special property is called "inheritance." It simply means that you inherit something from someone. When you inherit something, it is likely to be a couple of different things.

You are related to this person.

You might receive some biological trait like your hair type or nose.

These principles are the same when you use Ruby Programming language. There is a parent, grandparent, and even children classes. As a rule, children classes inherit the attributes of a parent or a grandparent class.

In Ruby, the grandparent of an object is known as the "superclass". In different words, should you have an object that is a string, this means that the object will inherit the properties of the string class. Then the parent of the class of the string is the string's "superclass". Ensure that you do not miss this important distinction. The superclass of the "string", which tells the program how to treat the strings, is not the same thing as the superclass. Here is an example:

```
1    > num1 = "this is a string"
```

| 2 | => "this is a string" |
|---|---|
| 3 | > num1.class |
| 4 | => String |
| 5 | > String.superclass |
| 6 | => Object |
| 7 | > Object.superclass |
| 8 | => BasicObject |
| 9 | > BasicObject.superclass |
| 10 | => nil |

What I have done is then set the local variable "num1" to be a "string". Once we look at the class of "num1", by calling ".class" method, it will tell us the class of "num1" is "string." When we look at the superclass of the "string", it will tell us the "object". Take a look at the effects of what would happen if I tried "num1.superclass":

1 > num1 = "this is a string"

2 => "this is a string"

3 > num1.superclass

4 => #<NoMethodError: undefined method `superclass' for "this is a string":String>

Notice the error. The reason why this does not work is because "num1" is considered to be an object. This means it has inherited the properties of the class "string", and that "num1" is not a class. This means that there is no superclass. Here is a different way of explaining what we just did:

1 > num1 = "this is a string"

2        => "this is a string"

3        > num1.class

4        => String

5        > num1.class.superclass

6        => Object

7        > num1.class.superclass.superclass

8        => BasicObject

9        > num1.class.superclass.superclass.superclass

10     => nil

The reason for the last value is because "BasicObject" has no parent, so we used "nil". It will inherit nothing from a different class. Therefore, it will stop there. One important thing to notice here is that there is a difference in the "chained" method. This means that it has continued to apply the method to the current statement. The amazing thing with Ruby is that it will evaluate something and return a copy to allow you to continue to view it. Look at the last line:

1        > num1.class.superclass.superclass.superclass

2        => nil

Ruby did this:

What is the class of "num1"? It is a string, so return to "string".

What is the superclass of the "string"? "String" is a child class of the "object", so go to "object".

What is the superclass of the "object"? "Object" is a child class of the "BasicObject", so return to the "BasicObject".

9

In order to put it all on one line with one command, you will need to follow the structure in the following code.

The structures of the classes and the superclasses are the hierarchy of the inheritance class. Now the question is; how is the class defined and how do you use it?

```
1    class MyClass
2        # some code logic
3    end
```

Basically, you will have an opening keyword ("class"), that is followed by the name of the class ("MyClass"). Then you will see your code, and then when you are finished, you will close it with the word "end". Ensure that the "class" and "end" are always lowercase. This is all there is to writing your code. If you have a "parent" class that you want it to inherit things from, you would type:

```
1    class MyChildClass < MyClass
2        # some code that is specific to the child class
3    end
```

Ruby will interpret the "<" operator to mean the class name is located on the right side. It is the parent class and the child is on the left. This means the child will inherit from the parent. Also, it is important to remember that the class names will start with an uppercase letter. If the name has multiple words, then you will not put a space between the words; for example, "CamelCasing".

Ruby Class Instances

Now you know how to create classes, which you now know are blueprints of an object. So, if you are thinking in the terms of baking, a class is almost like a recipe. Recipes contain a list of ingredients and some instructions in order to create the dish. Keeping this in mind, think of creating blueberry muffins. This means that each blueberry muffin is an instance of this class. So, each muffin (or instance) is an object. In order to create an instance, you will type:

```
1       muffin = BlueberryMuffin.new
```

You are doing great! The only part of the statement that is listed above that creates an instance of "BlueberryMuffin" class is the "BlueberryMuffin.new". To use the object you create, you will need to store it some place. So, it is stored in the local variable "muffin". This is so that it can be reused. You will then need to do more things with the class. For example, you will need to set up an initialization method. This is so that you can create an object of the class.

# Chapter 5: Data Structures in Ruby

In this chapter you will learn the structures of Ruby. This is an important part of learning Ruby. At the core of this programming language, it manipulates the data. Computer scientists have created a way to manipulate data using structure by inventing something called data structures. Data structures are containers for a certain type of data. Words are treated differently than formulas. Letters and characters are also treated differently than numbers, normally.

## Variables

A variable is a name of the basic type of container, which is used to store data. Each of the variables names are unique to its scope; the area that the variable is allowed to be stored. Think of it as a Venn diagram, which means that each and every variable is only valuable in a circle or a square that is in the container. For example, if you wanted to create a program that is responsible for adding a couple of numbers.

From the view of the coder, you will need to set up a certain container for each of those numbers. Then you will set up the mathematical function for both containers. The reason for this is because you do not want the user of the program to have to edit the code when they want to calculate the numbers. Most users know what a calculator is, so they can press buttons or enter the numbers. However, editing the code is not an option. In Ruby, every one of those containers is considered to be a variable. Therefore, you would type something like this:

```
1      sum = num1 + num2
```

Or you can type:

```
1      sum = 19 + 20
```

Ruby and other languages have different types of variables. Here are some types of variables.

**Local**:

This variable is only able to be used in a certain part of the program. Once it has exited that part, those variables are then destroyed. If you have a program that includes three methods, you could have the same variable (for example "num1") that is included in three different ways in each of the methods and stores three values. Going back into the Venn diagram, assume there are three shapes in the diagram; Circle 1, Circle 2, and a square. Also assume that Circle 1 and Circle 2 are not connected; yet both are inside the square. A local variable would be limited to its own circle and wouldn't be able to affect any aspect of the outside. The way to use this type of variable is to simply use them. If you are wanting to use a local variable called "sum", which will store the sum of the values of "num1", as well as "num2", you will simply write the codes as: sum = num1 + num2

**Global**:

This variable is used throughout the entire program. Going back into the Venn diagram, these specific variables would be considered the square. This way, if you need to access a variable that is outside of the circles, but still within the square, you can. You will use these in Ruby by typing "$" before its name. Assume you would like to calculate a multiple dimension circle; you will need to define the radius first. You will do it like this: "$radius = 20". Then at other times, through the program, no matter if you are in a sub circle of the square, you can reference to "$radius".

Using global variables has a good side, as well as a bad side. The good side is that you are able to read the value of them in any method or function using your program. The bad side is that you will also be able to write a global variable in any method or function in your program. If you end up changing the value, and forget the other method or function, you will completely mess things up. As a general rule, you should stay away from using global variables unless you are very confident that you know where they are to be used and how they change things in the program.

## Constants

These variables are considered to be "sacred" global variables. The values of this type of variable are to remain constant for the life of the program. If you wanted to specify a mathematical constant such as pi, you can easily use it throughout the program. You would type something like this: PI = 3.14. Constants must begin with an uppercase letter. It will typically always be uppercase through the whole thing. However, they can be changed here and there. Ruby does not forbid you from changing the value. However, when you do change it, it will give you a warning. Going into the Venn diagram again, think of "PI" as being outside of the square. It is able to be used anywhere inside the square or in the circles that are inside the square.

## Class

These variables have a scope that is limited to the class in which they are defined. Class variables are defined by "@@" in the beginning of the name.

## Instance

These variables have a scope that is limited to a particular instance of a certain class. They are defined using "@" at the beginning of the name.

## Local

Local variable names will start with a lowercase or an underscore.

Sum = num1 + num2

## Global

The global variable name will start with "$".

## Constants

Constants should always start with an uppercase letter; however, they are typically written in all caps.

PI = 3.14

## Class

@@length = 10 #

This will denote the length of the side of a specified object in a class. In this case there is an imaginary class titled "Square". The length of the sides are demonstrated for the purposes of learning. It is important to remember that all sides of a square are equal, and in this line of code it is 10 by default.

## Instance

@length = 5 #

This shows that the length of a side of an object is 5 instead of 10. You can also use this instance variable in order to specify the length of a specific square, like "Red Square".

## Reserve Words

These are words that you cannot use. They are reserved to be used internally in order to identify different elements of the language. These are:

- _FILE_
- _LINE_
- BEGIN
- END
- alias
- And
- Begin
- Break
- Case
- Class
- Def
- Defined?
- Do
- Else
- Elsif
- End

- Ensure
- False
- For
- If
- In
- Module
- Next
- Nil
- Not
- Or
- Redo
- Rescue
- Retry
- Return
- Self
- Super
- Then true
- Undef
- Unless
- Until
- When
- While

- Yield

**Ruby Strings**

A string is specified by a series or a sequence of characters; for example, a sequence of words. You may say a sentence; however, a string is not just any sentence. For example:

1    string1 = 'a'

2    string2 = 'This is a string'

Two things will happen here, the first is that local variables will be used, and then the second is that single quotes are used to define the content. Even though "string1" contains one letter, it is still considered a string due to it being declared in a single quote. Ruby understands that you must treat a variable by the way it is declared. You are able to use double quotes. However, you will need to be consistent. You cannot start a strings declaration with a double quote and end it with a single quote. For example:

string1 = "This is a string."

OR

String2 = 'This is also a string.'

Both ways are valid and it is all a matter of personal preference.

1    num1 = 9

This will set "num1" to the numerical value of 9. You can enter "num1 + 1", that means the result will end up being 10. But if you use single quotes around the number 9, like this:

```
1      num1 = '9'
```

This means that 9 is actually a string and not just a number. If you wrote num1 + 1, it would throw up an error with the lines of: => #. The interpreter is saying that you will give it a number and a string. It means it does not know how to add them together. To take this further, if you typed this:

```
1    num1 = '9'

2    num2 = '1'

3    num1 + num2
```

This coding would end up looking like this:

```
1      "91"
```

This is because Ruby will take the two strings and literally put them together. When the value is specified with quotes, you are telling the interpreter not to translate this. Just take the exact content between the quotes. It will treat the 9 like a letter. So, as far as the interpreter is concerned, it looks like this:

```
1      num1 = '9'
```

OR

```
1      num2 = 'a'
```

Here is another example. If you were to type num1 + num2, then your result will be "9s". In summary, strings are a combination of numbers, letters, and special characters.

# Chapter 6: Ruby Collections

Thus far, individual pieces of data have been covered. However, what happens if we would like to work with many pieces of data? I am speaking of a collection of a series of numbers that need to be put in ascending order. Or maybe a list of names that need to be sorted alphabetically. How does the Ruby program manage to do that? Ruby will provide two tools; hashes, as well as arrays.

## Arrays

The easiest way to understand and explain arrays is to show you an example. A typical one will look like this:

FOOD

| | |
|---|---|
| CHICKEN | [0] |
| RICE | [1] |
| STEAK | [2] |
| FISH | [3] |
| SHRIMP | [4] |
| BEEF | [5] |

Rather than having to have six different variables for the different food types, you can just have a food array that will store each of the food items in their own element or container. The numbers to the right are the "keys" or "index" of the elements. ([0] = chicken, [1] = rice, and so on) Note the keys are always numbers and always begin with 0 and go up from there. The first element will always be [0] and the second will always be [1], and so on. This means that the last of the elements is always the total length of the array minus 1. This is because you started at [0]. To create the above in your program, you will do something like this:

```
1    food = ['chicken', 'rice', 'steak', 'fish', 'shrimp', 'beef']
2    => ['chicken', 'rice', 'steak', 'fish', 'shrimp', 'beef']
3    > food.count
4    => 6
```

Notice that each element uses single quotes. This is because you are storing the strings in the elements. The array class has methods that you can use out of the box, like "count". It counts the number of elements in the array and will output the value. Thus, even though the index goes to 5, there are 6 elements. This is because the index begins at 0. Now that you have created the food array, you can use each item by invoking the name followed by the index number.

```
1    > food[0]
2    => "chicken"
3    > food[1]
4    => "rice"
5    > food[2]
6    => "steak"
7    > food[6]
8    => nil
```

The reason you get "nil" at "food [6]" is due to there being no [6], or rather there is nothing stored in that spot. Ruby will automatically set "food [6]", "food [7]", and so on to "nil". In order to add another food item to the array, you just have to set the next element. For example:

```
1   > food[6] = 'carrots'
2   => "carrots"
3   > food
4   => ["chicken", "rice", "steak", "fish", "shrimp", "beef", "carrots"]
5   > food.count
6   => 7
```

There is another way you can add new elements to the array. You can use the append operator ( << ). This will basically stick something at the end of your array. The difference is that you don to have to specify an index position when you use the append operator. Here is an example:

```
1   > food << "irish potato"
2   => ["chicken", "rice", "steak", "fish", shrimp", "beef", "carrots", "irish potato"]
3   > food << 42
4   => ["chicken", "rice", "steak", "fish", "shrimp", "beef", "carrots", "irish potato", 42]
```

Everything that comes after the "<<" is then added into the array. This is convenient due to the ability to append variables and objects to the array without having to worry about the content. For example:

```
1   > sum = 10 + 23
2   => 33
```

3   > food << sum

4   => ["chicken", "rice", "steak", "fish", "shrimp", "beef",
"carrots", "irish potato", 42, 33]

All you need here is to create a local variable named "sum",
and then you will push the value of "sum" to the end of your
array. You will then add arrays to the end of other arrays:

1  > name_and_age = ["Marc", "Gayle", 28]

2  => ["Marc", "Gayle", 28]

3  > food

4   => ["chicken", "rice", "steak", "fish", "shrimp", "beef",
"carrots", "irish potato", 42, 33]

5  > food.count

6  => 10

7  > food << name_and_age

8   => ["chicken", "rice", "steak", "fish", "shrimp", "beef",
"carrots", "irish potato", 42, 33, ["Marc", "Gayle", 28]]

9  > food.last

10  => ["Marc", "Gayle", 28]

11  > food.count

12  =>11

Even though the last elemtent in your array has three
elements, it will still count it as one element. The count
figure then goes from 10 to 11. If you want to find out how
many elements are inside the last element of the array, you
can do this:

```
1    > food.last.count
2    => 3
```

There are a few other interesting methods that you can use right out of the box like "first", "last", "length", "include?", "empty?", "eql?", and "sort".

```
1    > food
2    => ["chicken", "rice", "steak", "fish", "shrimp",
     "beef", "carrots"]
3    > food.first
4    => "chicken"
5    > food.last
6    => "carrots"
7    > food.length
8    => 7
9    > food.count
10   => 7
11   > food.include?("chicken")
12   => true
13   > food.include?("filet mignon")
14   => false
15   > food.empty?
16   => false
17   > food[0]
18   => "chicken"
19   > food[0].eql?("chicken")
20   => true
```

```
21    > food[0].eql?("beef")
22    => false
23    > food.sort
24    => ["beef", "carrots", "chicken", "fish", "rice",
      "shrimp", "steak"]
```

Inside the brackets to the right after "eql?", there is a string in double quotes. This is because you are dealing with a string. Also, "sort" arranges it alphabetically and from the lowest to the highest of numbers. You can store anything in the elements, not just the strings. You can mix some elements as well. If you would like an array of numbers, then you can use something like this:

```
1     numbers = [1, 2, 3, 4, 5, 6]
2     => [1, 2, 3, 4, 5, 6]
```

Remember earlier when I said that you should always start with the index at "0"? You will be able to see in this code that this is extremely important. In this order, number "1" is referenced as [0]. This is due to it being the very first element in your array.

```
1     > numbers[0]
2     => 1
3     > numbers[1]
4     => 2
5     > numbers[6]
6     => nil
7     > numbers.first
```

8       => 1

9       > numbers.last

10      => 6

11      > numbers.count

12      => 6

13      > numbers.length

14      => 6

15      > numbers.include?(3)

16      => true

17      > numbers.include?(10)

18      => false

19      > numbers.empty?

20      => false

21      > numbers[1]

22      => 2

23      > numbers[1].eql?(1)

24      => false

25      > numbers[1].eql?(2)

        => true

Since you are evaluating numbers, the objects that are located in the brackets should be wrapped in the double quotes. They should be used like this:

1       > numbers.include?("3")

2       => false

3       > numbers[1].eql?("2")

4     => false

Everything that you have just read about covers a one-dimensional array. These are arrays with just one column. These are good to be used to store different types of lists of items. You can use multi-dimensional arrays as well. Here is an example of a 2-D array. Once you have grasped this, then you can move on to more dimensions. Here is a 2-D array:

| | | | |
|---|---|---|---|
| [0][0] ← | CHICKEN | 10 | → [0][1] |
| [1][0] ← | RICE | 5 | → [1][1] |
| [2][0] ← | STEAK | 20 | → [2][1] |
| [3][0] ← | FISH | 15 | → [3][1] |
| [4][0] ← | SHRIMP | 18 | → [4][1] |
| [5][0] ← | BEEF | 9 | → [5][1] |

There are two things being stored: the name of each dish, along with the price that is related to the items. As the coding suggests, in order to have access to the elements, you will use both keys. This is how this is done:

1   > food2 = [["chicken", 10], ["rice", 5], ["steak", 20], ["fish", 15], ["shrimp", 18], ["beef", 9]]

2   => [["chicken", 10], ["rice", 5], ["steak", 20], ["fish", 15], ["shrimp", 18], ["beef", 9]]

A few differences between the keys will jump out at you. Essentially, "food2" is an array of an array. This means that this I an array whose elements are actually arrays. Look at the elements here:

1   > food2[0]

2   => ["chicken", 10]

3   > food2[1]

4    => ["rice", 5]

5    > food2[2]

6    => ["steak", 20]

7    > food2[3]

8    => ["fish", 15]

When you have access to each single element, you will notice each has an array inside. For an example, ["chicken", 10] is an array that includes a string (chicken) in the first of the elements and the number is 10 in the second elements. To access the elements, you will do this:

1    > food2[0]

2    => ["chicken", 10]

3    > food2[0][0]

4    => "chicken"

5    > food2[0][1]

6    => 10

Firstly, food2 [ 0 ] [ 0 ] is saying that the first element is the first element of the specified array food2), and then food2 [ 0 ] [ 1 ] is saying that the second element is of the first element of the array food2. You can also use methods that are the same class array on sub-arrays. Take a look at this:

1  > food2

2  => [["chicken", 10], ["rice", 5], ["steak", 20], ["fish",

3  15], ["shrimp", 18], ["beef", 9]]

4  > food2.count

5 => 6

6 > food2[0]

7 => ["chicken", 10]

8 > food2[0].count

9 => 2

10> food2.last

11 => ["beef", 9]

12> food2.first

   => ["chicken", 10]


Keep in mind that there is one important difference for multi-dimensional arrays. Ruby will check what you call a method. For instance, if you would like to check whether "chicken" is in the "food2" array, you will not be able to do this:

1    > food2.include?("chicken")

2    => false


The reasoning is that "food2" is just an array of another array. So, you will have to do this:

1  > food2

2  => [["chicken", 10], ["rice", 5], ["steak", 20], ["fish", 15], ["shrimp", 18], ["beef", 9]]

3  > food2[0].include?("chicken")

4  => true

You would have had to specify the specific element ( [0] ) that you wanted to check for a string (chicken). In this case, you know that the string "chicken" was stored in the "food2 [ 0 ]".

# Chapter 7: Ruby Iterators, Blocks, and Hashes

An iterator is a mechanism in the Ruby program that will enable you to go through data structures, which store multiple elements like arrays. It will also examine all elements. One of the most typically used methods is named "each". Each is a certain method in a specified array class that will come with Ruby. We will begin with simple coding. Imagine if you want to print a list of the food items that you stored in the "food" array. This is how you would accomplish this:

```
1      > food
2      => ["chicken", "rice", "steak", "fish", "beef"]
3
4      food.each do |x|
5      puts x
6      end
7
8      chicken
9      rice
10     steak
11     fish
12     beef
```

A few things that you should be aware of are:

1.  You will only be able to call "each" on a collection of data.

2.  Once you use the call "each", you will pass the block to it. A block is a contained bit of code. Simply put, you are telling it to apply the code contained in the block to "each" element that you are looking at.

## Blocks

There are two different ways to use a block. The first is much similar to the example listed above, where you will just enter this code:

```
1    do |variable| #some code end
```

You should see that you used a block with an iterator. You will be able to define a block outside of the iterator; however, in order to execute the block, you will have to use it with an iterator. That is why it said do |x| after each food earlier. You will then be able to use one or even more variables in the block. Those variables are local to the block. This means that they will be destroyed after you leave. This also means that if you have two blocks, you can use the variable x in both of them, and one will not affect the other. In the example that is provided above about the food, each element of the array "food", is printed to the screen. Another way to use the block is on one line like this bit of coding:

```
1    food.each { |x| puts x }
```

In this specific case, the opening curly brace 9 { ) replaces the "do", and then the closing curly brace ( } ) will replace the "end". If the operation is just one line, then it will conveniently find the rereading of such a code in the future.

Usually, just use "do" and "end" to make it easier. However, again this is also due to personal preference.

The reason that a block uses variables, it is because the elements of this collection are to not be modified; of course, unless you specify to do so. Basically, what will happen is that every single iteration through the array, a copy of the element is stored in "x", and then "x" is also used in the block. Going through the "food" array, the local block of variable "x" would look like this:

First iteration:

```
1    food[0] = 'chicken'

2    x = food[0]

3    x = 'chicken'
```

Second iteration:

```
1    food[1] = 'rice'

2    x = food[1]

3    x = 'rice'
```

Third iteration:

```
1    food[2] = 'steak'

2    x = food[2]

3    x = 'steak'
```

Using numbers would be more clearly illustrate that the values are not changed in the first array:

```
1        > numbers = [1, 2, 3, 4, 5]

2        => [1, 2, 3, 4, 5]

3        > numbers.each do |x|

4        ... x = x + 2

5        ... puts x
```

| 6 | ... end |
|---|---|
| 7 | |
| 8 | 3 |
| 9 | 4 |
| 10 | 5 |
| 11 | 6 |
| 12 | 7 |
| 13 | |
| 14 | > numbers |
| 15 | => [1, 2, 3, 4, 5] |

Here you have printed out numbers 3, 4, 5, 6, 7, (1+2, 2+2, 3+2, and on), but in the end, the "numbers" array is in identical.

## Ruby Hashes

A Ruby hash is yet another collection type. It is a collection of key value pairs. A key value pair is a combination of the title of a container and the contents of the specified container.

1  a => "Marc"

In this key value pair, the key is "a" and the value is "Marc". A hash is a list of these key value pairs, they are separated using commas. A hash looks this way:

1    a =>"Marc", b => "Cheyenne", c => "Alexander", d=> "Mia"

Arrays and hashes have some important differences.

The keys are not integers keys. They are characters, strings, integers, and so on. This is any type of object.

The keys are not in order. You could not just say that "a" is "first" or that it will come before "b" in the example above. This is because the program doesn't look at the order of the keys in the hashes.

Even though some keys are not in order, you were iterating using the hash. Ruby will go though them and order them. In the example, if you were printing out the value, the program will print out "marc", "Cheyenne", etc. Do not confuse this with the way an array key is ordered.

There are different ways to initialize a hash. However, the typical way looks like this:

```
1      > day = Hash.new
2      => {}
```

In order to create a hash with certain values:

```
1   > names = Hash["a" => "Marc", "b" => "Cheyenne", "c"
=> "Alexander", "d" => "Mia"]

2    => {"a"=>"Marc", "b"=>"Cheyenne", "c"=>"Alexander",
"d"=>"Mia"}

3   > names2 = {"a" => "Marc", "b" => "Cheyenne"}

4   => {"a" => "Marc", "b" =>"Cheyenne"}
```

You will see that in order to create the hash, you do not have to use the "Hash" keyword or square brackets. You are able to use them if you want to or you can just type this: = { }. For the specific keys and the values, you also do not need to put the keys inside quotes. You need to do this only should you want to use strings as keys. Ruby will also require a =>

(called "rocket") in order to assign the value on the right side of the rocket to the key that is on the left. If you tried to do "names2" while not using quotes around the keys, you would see an error like this one:

```
1  > names2 = { a => "Marc", b => "Cheyenne"}

2  => #<NameError: undefined local variable or method `a'
   for main:Object>
```

In order to access the values in the hash, you will need to specify the names of the hash, as well as the key for the values you try to access:

```
   > names
1
   =>            {"a"=>"Marc",        "b"=>"Cheyenne",
2  "c"=>"Alexander", "d"=>"Mia"}

3  > names["a"]

4  => "Marc"

5  > names["c"]

6  => "Alexander"

7  > names[a]

8  => #<NameError: undefined local variable or method
   `a' for main:Object>
```

Since you did not use quotes for "names [ a ]", then the interpreter will think that "a" is a local variable or method. It will not be able to find the value for it. Therefore, it will throw an error up. If you tried to gain access that seems legitimate, to a legitimate key that has not been assigned to a value, then Ruby will usually return "nil".

```
1  > day["a"]
```

2  => nil

3  > day[9]

4  => nil  #For you Day9 fans, don't worry... I am a fan too
<img                      src="https://hackhands.com/wp-
includes/images/smilies/icon_smile.gif" alt=":)" class="wp-
smiley">

Assume that you would like to create a hash in which every single value has a default value. You can do this:

1    > year = Hash.new("2012")

2    => {}

3    > year[0]

4    => "2012"

5    > year[12]

6    => "2012"

All you have done is call the method "new" on the Ruby class "hash" and pass the default value of "2012" to the method. When trying to gain access to the value that does not exist, instead of returning a "nil", the program will return the default value ( 2012 ". You will be able to use different methods with hashes:

1    > names.keys

2    => ["a", "b", "c", "d", "e"]

3    > names.values

4    => ["Marc", "Cheyenne", "Alexander", "Mia", "Christopher"]

As you may have guessed, the "keys" just return all the keys inside the hash, and the "values" return the values.

```
1  > names.length

2  => 5

3  > names.has_key?("a")

4  => true

5  > names.has_key?("z")

6  => false

7  > names.has_key("a")

8  => #<NoMethodError: undefined method `has_key' for
   #<Hash:0x55c797d7>>
```

Note that "has_key" method has the name of "has_key?". If you left the "?" out, then it will throw an error like the one above. All that "has_key?" is doing is checking the hash to see if any keys may match what is in the brackets. If the program finds a match, then it will return "true"; if it does not, then the return is "false".

All you have done above was created a new hash, "f_names", by assigning the existing names "hash". Then, you created another hash, "1_names", that has a few different last names. Then, you merged the two hashes in order to create a master hash. But because you ran the "merge" method without assigning the result to a variable, it was not stored. If you check the values of the "f_name" and "1_names" after, you will then see they look the same as before you ran the "merge". If you want to store the value of that merge, you will have to have something like this:

```
1  > master_hash = f_names.merge(l_names)
```

2    => {"a"=>"Marc", "b"=>"Cheyenne", "c"=>"Alexander", "d"=>"Mia",          "e"=>"Christopher",          "g"=>"Gayle", "h"=>"Gayle", "j"=>"Jackson", "m"=>"Brown"}

A different approach is to do a "destructive" merge. This is a great feature of Ruby. For many methods, should you add an exclamation point to the end of a method call, you will replace the value of the method caller with a returned value. Take a look at this:

1  > f_names

2    => {"a"=>"Marc", "b"=>"Cheyenne", "c"=>"Alexander", "d"=>"Mia", "e"=>"Christopher"}

3  > l_names

4      => {"g"=>"Gayle", "h"=>"Gayle", "j"=>"Jackson", "m"=>"Brown"}

5  > f_names.merge!(l_names)

6    => {"a"=>"Marc", "b"=>"Cheyenne", "c"=>"Alexander", "d"=>"Mia",          "e"=>"Christopher",          "g"=>"Gayle", "h"=>"Gayle", "j"=>"Jackson", "m"=>"Brown"}

7  > f_names

8    => {"a"=>"Marc", "b"=>"Cheyenne", "c"=>"Alexander", "d"=>"Mia",          "e"=>"Christopher",          "g"=>"Gayle", "h"=>"Gayle", "j"=>"Jackson", "m"=>"Brown"}

As you are able to see here, the "f_names" value ran the destructive merge method ( merge! ) is now the same value as the hash that was merged. Another method is that you are able to use the hashes as "each". However, it is different. With the arrays, you will have to pass this in one variable to a black. With the hashes, you will pass the two variables; one that will represent the key, and the other that will represent the value.

```
1  > f_names.each do |key, value|

2  .. puts "#{key} is #{value}"

3  .. end

4  => "a is Marcb is Cheyennec is Alexanderd is Miae is
Christopherg is Gayleh is Gaylej is Jacksonm is Brown"
```
This does look messy. Here is what is happening in this line of coding:

- Reading from the left to the right, Ruby will read the left first and the oldest value first. It stores these values in "key" and "value". Therefore,
- after the first iteration, :key" would be "a", and the "value" would be "Marc".
- Then, the program will go inside the block and execute it top down. The first command that is listed is "puts", followed with a string. In different words, it will then print everything in quote to the screen.
- The syntax inside the quotes is the "puts" and is called a string interpolation. It says to stick to the value of the variable into the string at that exact point. Therefore, after the first iteration, "puts" will do this:
- Looks for the key variable.
- Print the variable to the screen.
- Print a space. This is because you put a space in between the key and the "is".
- Print the next word.
- Print another space.
- Print the value variable "Marc".
- Go to the next command because this command is done.

- Sees "end", then goes back to the beginning of the specified block in order to see if there are any more elements that are in the hash object.
- Sine it is in a block, it will repeat this entire process for each key value pair that is in the hash until there aren't any more.
- Sine you did not add a space before the last double quotes on the "puts" line, there is no space will be between the last character of the first iteration, as well as the first character of the second iteration.
- In different words, if "puts" looks like "puts " #{key} is #{value}", then the resulting string will make more sense: a is Marc b is Cheyenne c is Alexander, and so on.

# Chapter 8: Ruby Symbols

A Ruby symbol is also an object type. It resembles a string; however, it is not quite a string. The one major difference is that a symbol will always begin with a colon ( :name). Symbols work well with hashes. This is because you are able to use them like keys instead of strings. Take a look at this:

1  > f_names

2  => {:a =>"Marc", :b =>"Cheyenne", :c =>"Alexander", :d =>"Mia", :e =>"Christopher"}

3  > f_names[:a]

4  => "Marc"

The wonderful thing about this is that you will no longer have to worry about the quotes for both the values and the keys.

1  > pets = {:dog => "Cookie", :cat => "Snowy", :fish => "Goldie"}

2  => {:dog=>"Cookie", :cat=>"Snowy", :fish=>"Goldie"}

3  > pets[:dog]

4  => "Cookie"

5  > pets[:fish]

6  => "Goldie"

Symbols will make messing with hashes a lot simpler than using the strings as keys. You can also use hashes for anything else in the program. Their main function is to store the values and make retrieval a lot easier for the interpreter.

# Chapter 9: Samples of Ruby Coding

Within this chapter you will be given samples of many different pieces of coding in the Ruby program that you can use.

## Sample of a String

# Double-quoted strings can substitute variables.

a = 17

print "a = #{a}\n";

print 'a = #{a}\n';

print "\n";

# If you're verbose, you can create a multi-line string like this:

b = <<ENDER

This is a longer string,

perhaps some instructions or agreement

goes here.  By the way,

a = #{a}.

ENDER

print "\n[[[" + b + "]]]\n";

```
print "\nActually, any string
```

can span lines.  The line\nbreaks just become part of the string.
"

```
print %Q=\nThe highly intuitive "%Q" prefix allows
```
alternative delimiters.\n=

```
print %Q[Bracket symbols match their mates, not
```
themselves.\n]

## Sample Array

```
a = [ 45, 3, 19, 8 ]
b = [ 'sam', 'max', 56, 98.9, 3, 10, 'jill' ]
print (a + b).join(' '), "\n"
print a[2], " ", b[4], " ", b[-2], "\n"
print a.sort.join(' '), "\n"
a << 57 << 9 << 'phil'
print "A: ", a.join(' '), "\n"

b << 'alex' << 48 << 220
print "B: ", b.join(' '), "\n"
print "pop: ", b.pop, "\n"
print "shift: ", b.shift, "\n"
print "C: ", b.join(' '), "\n"

b.delete_at(2)
b.delete('alex')
print "D: ", b.join(' '), "\n"
```

## Sample Hash

```
z = { 'mike' => 75, 'bill' => 18, 'alice' => 32 }
z['joe'] = 44
print z['bill'], " ", z['joe'], " ", z["smith"], "\n"
print z.has_key?('mike'), " ", z.has_key?("jones"), "\n"
```

## Sample Iterators

```
# Here's a different way to add up an array:

fred = [ 4, 19, 3, 7, 32 ]
sum = 0
fred.each { |i| sum += i }
print "Sum of [", fred.join(" "), "] is #{sum}\n"


# Or create a secret message:

key = { 'A' => 'U', 'B' => 'Q', 'C' => 'A', 'D' => 'F', 'E' =>
'D', 'F' => 'K',
    'G' => 'P', 'H' => 'W', 'I' => 'N', 'J' => 'L', 'K' => 'J',
'L' => 'M',
    'M' => 'S', 'N' => 'V', 'O' => 'Y', 'P' => 'O', 'Q' => 'Z',
'R' => 'T',
    'S' => 'E', 'T' => 'I', 'U' => 'X', 'V' => 'B', 'W' => 'G',
'X' => 'H',
    'Y' => 'R', 'Z' => 'C' }
```

```ruby
print "\nThe encoded message is: "
"The secret message".each_byte do | b |
   b = b.chr.upcase
   if key.has_key?(b) then
      print key[b]
   else
      print b
   end
end
print "\n"


# But give us the info to read it anyway.
print "The key is: "
ct = 8
key.each { | k, v |
   if ct == 8 then
      print "\n   "
      ct = 0
   else
      print ", "
   end
   ct = ct + 1
   print "#{v} => #{k}"
}
```

```
print "\n\n"

# Some interesting things from Integer.
3.times { print "Hi! " }
print "\n"

print "Count: "
3.upto(7) { |n| print n, " " }
print "\n"
```

## Sample Class

```
# Class names must be capitalized.  Technically, it's a
constant:
class Fred

  # The initialize method is the constructor.  The @val is
  # an object value.
  def initialize(v)
    @val = v
  end

  # Set it and get it.
  def set(v)
    @val = v
  end
```

```ruby
  def get
    return @val
  end
end


# Objects are created by the new method of the class
object.
a = Fred.new(10)
b = Fred.new(22)


print "A: ", a.get, " ", b.get,"\n";
b.set(34)
print "B: ", a.get, " ", b.get,"\n";


# Ruby classes are always unfinished works.  This does not
# re-define Fred, it adds more stuff to it.
class Fred
  def inc
    @val += 1
  end
end


a.inc
b.inc
```

```
print "C: ", a.get, " ", b.get,"\n";

# Objects may have methods all to themselves.
def b.dec
  @val -= 1
end

begin
  b.dec
  a.dec
rescue StandardError => msg
  print "Error: ", msg, "\n"
end

print "D: ", a.get, " ", b.get,"\n";
```

## Sample Inheritance

```
# Class names must be capitalized.  Technically, it's a
constant.
class Fred

  # The initialize method is the constructor.  The @val is
  # an object value.
  def initialize(v)
    @val = v
```

```ruby
  end

  # Set it and get it.
  def set(v)
    @val = v
  end

  def get
    return @val
  end

  def more(y)
    @val += y
  end

  def less(y)
    @val -= y
  end

  def to_s
    return "Fred(val=" + @val.to_s + ")"
  end
end
```

# Class Barney is derived from Fred with the usual meaning.

```ruby
class Barney < Fred
 def initialize(x)
   super(x)
   @save = x
 end

 def chk
   @save = @val
 end

 def restore
   @val = @save
 end

 def to_s
   return "(Backed-up) " + super + " [backup value: " +
@save.to_s + "]"
 end

end
```

# Objects are created by the new method of the class object.

```
a = Fred.new(398)
b = Barney.new(112)

a.more(34)
b.more(817)

print "A: a = ", a, "\n  b = ", b, "\n";

a.more(34)
b.more(817)

print "B: a = ", a, "\n  b = ", b, "\n";

b.chk

a.more(34)
b.more(817)

print "C: a = ", a, "\n  b = ", b, "\n";

b.restore

print "D: a = ", a, "\n  b = ", b, "\n";
```

# Sample Box Class

```
# Box drawing class.
class Box
  # Initialize to given size, and filled with spaces.
  def initialize(w,h)
    @wid = w
    @hgt = h
    @fill = ' '
  end

  # Change the fill.
  def fill(f)
    @fill = f
    return self
  end

  # Rotate 90 degrees.
  def flip
    @wid, @hgt = @hgt, @wid
    return self
  end

  # Generate (print) the box
```

```ruby
def gen
  line('+', @wid - 2, '-')
  (@hgt - 2).times { line('|', @wid - 2, @fill) }
  line('+', @wid - 2, '-')
end


# For printing
def to_s
  fill = @fill
  if fill == ' '
    fill = '(spaces)'
  end
  return "Box " + @wid.to_s + "x" + @hgt.to_s + ", filled: " + fill
end

private
  # Print one line of the box.
  def line(ends, count, fill)
    print ends;
    count.times { print fill }
    print ends, "\n";
  end
end
```

```
# Create some boxes.
b1 = Box.new(10, 4)
b2 = Box.new(5,12).fill('$')
b3 = Box.new(3,3).fill('@')
print "b1 = ", b1, "\nb2 = ", b2, "\nb3 = ", b3, "\n\n"
# Print some boxes.
print "b1:\n";
b1.gen
print "\nb2:\n";
b2.gen
print "\nb3:\n";
b3.gen
print "\nb2 flipped and filled with #:\n";
b2.fill('#').flip.gen
print "\nb2 = ", b2, "\n"
```

## Sample Method 1

```
# Square the number
def sqr(x)
    return x*x
end
# See how it works.
(rand(4) + 2).times {
```

```
  a = rand(300)
  print a,"^2 = ", sqr(a), "\n"
}
print "\n"
# Don't need a parm.
def boom
  print "Boom!\n"
end
boom
boom
# Default parms
print "\n"
def line(cnt, ender = "+", fill = "-")
  print ender, fill * cnt, ender, "\n"
end
line(8)
line(5,'*')
line(11,'+','=')
# Do they change?
def incr(n)
  n = n + 1
end
a = 5
incr(a)
```

```
print a,"\n"
```

## Sample Method 2

```
# Place the array in a random order.  Floyd's alg.
def shuffle(arr)
  for n in 0...arr.size
    targ = n + rand(arr.size - n)
    arr[n], arr[targ] = arr[targ], arr[n] if n != targ
  end
end
# Make strange declarations.
def pairs(a, b)
  a << 'Insane'
  shuffle(b)
  b.each { |x| shuffle(a); a.each { |y| print y, " ", x, ".\n"
}}
end
first = ['Strange', 'Fresh', 'Alarming']
pairs(first,    ['lemonade',    'procedure',    'sounds',
'throughway'])
print "\n", first.join(" "), "\n"
```

## Sample Method 3

```
# Add the strings before and after around each parm
and print
def surround(before, after, *items)
```

```ruby
  items.each { |x| print before, x, after, "\n" }
end

surround('[', ']', 'this', 'that', 'the other')
print "\n"

surround('<', '>', 'Snakes', 'Turtles', 'Snails',
'Salamanders', 'Slugs',
    'Newts')
print "\n"

def boffo(a, b, c, d)
  print "a = #{a} b = #{b}, c = #{c}, d = #{d}\n"
end
# Use * to adapt between arrays and arguments
a1 = ['snack', 'fast', 'junk', 'pizza']
a2 = [4, 9]
boffo(*a1)
boffo(17, 3, *a2)
```

## Sample of Setting Variables

```ruby
# Class names must be capitalized.  Technically, it's a
constant.
class Fred
```

```ruby
# The initialize method is the constructor.  The @val is
# an object value.
def initialize(v)
  @val = v
end


# Set it and get it.
def set(v)
  @val = v
end

def to_s
  return "Fred(val=" + @val.to_s + ")"
end


# Since a simple access function is so common, ruby
lets you declare one
# automatically, like this:
attr_reader :val
# You can list any number of object variables. Separate
by commas, and each
# needs its own colon
# attr_reader :fred, :joe, :alex, :sally
end
```

```ruby
class Alice <Fred
  # We have a message, too.
  def initialize(n, m)
    super(n)
    @msg = m
  end

  # Takes the base result and changes the class name.
  def to_s
    ret = super
    ret.gsub!(/Fred/, 'Alice')
    return ret + ' ' + @msg + '!'
  end
  # The = allows the method to be used on the right, and
  the left of the
  # assignment is the parameter.
  def appmsg=(more)
    @msg += more
  end


  # Like attr_reader, if you want the data to be
  assignable.
  attr_writer :msg
end
```

```
a = Fred.new(45)
b = Alice.new(11, "So there")

print "A: a = ", a, "\n  b = ", b, "\n"

print "B: ", a.val, " ", b.val, "\n"

b.msg = "Never"
print "B: b = ", b, "\n"
b.appmsg = " In a million years"
print "C: b = ", b, "\n"
```

## Sample Gate Classes

```
#
# Ruby circuit simulation classes.  This file contains a
base class Gate,
# and several derived classes describing digital logic
gates.  There are
# also classes for input and display.  There's also a flip-
flop.
#


class Gate
  # This is a count of the "active" gates, which are ones
  which have received
```

```
# a signal but not resolved it.
@@active = 0


# This is a list of gates which have registered that they
want to be
# notified when the circuit is quiet.  They give an
integer priority,
# and are notified in increasing priority order.
@@needquiet = { }
def quiet_register(pri)
  if ! @@needquiet.key?(pri) then @@needquiet[pri] =
[ ] end
  @@needquiet[pri].push(self)
end


# Here's how we set stuff.  There are static and object
versions of
# each, since I may want to activate from other spots.
def Gate.activate
  @@active += 1
end
def activate
  Gate.activate
end
def Gate.deactivate
```

```ruby
      @@active -= 1
      if @@active == 0 then
        @@needquiet.keys.sort.each \
              { |p| @@needquiet[p].each { |g| g.onquiet } }
      end
    end
  end
  def deactivate
    Gate.deactivate
  end


  # This is the default quiet action (nothing).
  def onquiet
  end


  # A signal is directed to a particular port on a
particular gate.  This
  # encapsulates those two data.  When a gate connects
to us, we send back
  # one of these to direct its later signal changes.
  class LinkHandle
    def initialize(sink_gate, sink_port)
      @sinkg = sink_gate
      @sinkp = sink_port
    end
```

```ruby
  # The sending gate uses this method to forward the signal to the
  # downstream gate.
  def signal(value)
    @sinkg.signal(@sinkp,value)
  end


  attr_reader :sinkg, :sinkp
end


def initialize(ival = false)
  @inputs = [ ]      # Array of inputs (boolean values)
  @outputs = [ ]        # Array of LinkHandle objects where to send output
  @outval = ival     # Present output value.
end


# This is called when a input gate sends us a signal on a particular input.
# We recompute our output value, and, if it changes, we send it on to all
# of our outbound connections.
def signal(port, val)
  # The derived class needs to implement the value method.
```

```
    self.activate
    @inputs[port] = val
    newval = self.value
    if newval != @outval then
      @outval = newval
      @outputs.each { | c | c.signal(newval) }
    end
    self.deactivate
  end

  # Call this to connect your output to the next one of our
inputs.
  def connect(v)
    port = @inputs.length
    @inputs.push(v)
    c = LinkHandle.new(self, port)
    self.signal(port, v)
    return c
  end

  # Join me to another gate.
  def join(g)
    @outputs.push(g.connect(@outval))
  end
```

```ruby
def joinmany(*p)
  p.each { |i| self.join(i); }
end


attr_reader :outval


# Some printing help
def name
  return self.class.to_s
end
def insstr
  return (if @inputs.length == 0 then "-" else
@inputs.join('.') end)
end
def to_s
  return name + " " + insstr + " => " + @outval.to_s
end


# Create another object of the same type.
def another
  return self.class.new
end
def manyothers(n)
  ret = []
```

```
  n.times { ret.push(self.another) }
  return ret
 end


 # This manufactures any number of objects.  It is a
static method, and
 # inherited by the real gates.  The expression self.new,
then, runs the
 # new method on the actual object, which the
inheriting class.  Therefore,
 # it will create any gate.
 def Gate.many(n)
  ret = [ ]
  n.times { ret.push(self.new) }
  return ret
 end


 # Dump a whole circuit.  Yecch.
 def outlinks
  return @outputs
 end
 def Gate.dump(*roots)
  ct = -1
  gatemap = { }
  for g in roots
```

```
    gatemap[g] = (ct += 1) unless gatemap.has_key?(g)
  end

  printed = { }
  while roots.length > 0
   g = roots.shift
   next if printed.has_key?(g)
   print "[", gatemap[g], "] ", g, ":"
   for c in g.outlinks
     og = c.sinkg
     gatemap[og]    =    (ct    +=    1)    unless
gatemap.has_key?(og)
     print " ", gatemap[og], "@", c.sinkp
     roots.push(og)
   end
   print " [none]" if g.outlinks.length <= 0
   print "\n"
   printed[g] = true
  end
 end
end

# Standard and gate
class AndGate < Gate
```

```ruby
  def initialize
    super(true)
  end
  def value
    for i in @inputs
      return false if !i
    end
    return true
  end
end
class NandGate < AndGate
  def value
    return ! super
  end
end

# Standard or gate
class OrGate < Gate
  def value
    for i in @inputs
      return true if i
    end
    return false
  end
```

```ruby
end
class NorGate < OrGate
  def value
    return ! super
  end
end


# Standard xor gate
class XorGate < Gate
  def value
    ret = false
    for i in @inputs
      ret ^= i
    end
    return ret
  end
end


# Gates with a limited number of input connections.
class LimitedGate < Gate
  def initialize(max=1,i=false)
    super(i)
    @max = max
  end
```

```ruby
  # Enforce connect limit.
  def connect(v)
    if @inputs.length >= @max then
      raise TypeError.new("Too many input connections.")
    end
    super(v)
  end

end

# Not gate.
class NotGate < LimitedGate
  def initialize
    super(1,true)
  end
  def value
    return ! @inputs[0]
  end
end

# This is a "yes gate" or amplifier.  It just forwards its input to all its
# outputs
class Connector < LimitedGate
```

```ruby
def value
  return @inputs[0]
end


# We can also use it as a one-bit input device.
def send(v)
  self.signal(0,v)
end
end


# D Flip-Flop.  Level-triggered.  First input is D, second
is clock.
class FlipFlop < LimitedGate
  def initialize
    super(2)
  end
  def value
    return (if @inputs[1] then @inputs[0] else @outval
end)
  end
end


# D Flip-Flop.  Edge-triggered.  First input is D, second
is clock.
# I think the level-triggered might make a lot more
```

sense with this

```
# simulation, though these are better in circuits.
class FlipFlopET < FlipFlop
  def initialize
    super
    @newval = false
  end
  def value
    return @newval
  end
  def signal(port, val)
    # Need to stick our fingers in this thing to find the
rising edge.
    self.activate
    @newval =
      if port == 1 && !@inputs[1] && val then @inputs[0]
else @outval  end
    super(port,val)
    self.deactivate
  end
end


# Simple test point
class Tester < LimitedGate
  def initialize(name="Tester")
```

```ruby
  super(1)
  @name = name
 end
 attr_writer :name
 def value
   print @name, ": ", if @inputs[0] then "on" else "off"
end, "\n";
   return @inputs[0]
 end
end
# Numeric output device.  Connect lines starting with
LSB.
class NumberOut < Gate
 @@quiet = false
 def NumberOut.shush(q=true)
  @@quiet = q
 end

 def initialize(name="Value", pri = 1)
  @name = name
  quiet_register(pri)
  super()
 end

 attr_writer :name
```

```ruby
# Print the value on quiet.
def onquiet
  return if @@quiet;

  val = 0
  @inputs.reverse_each { |i|
    val <<= 1
    if i then
      val |= 1
    end
  }

  print @name, ": ", val, "\n"
end
def value
  return false
end
end

# LED which prints when circuit becomes quiet.
class LED < NumberOut
  def initialize(name="LED", pri = 1)
    super(name, pri)
  end
```

```ruby
  def onquiet
    if @inputs.length > 0 && ! @@quiet then
      print @name, ": ", if @inputs[0] then "on" else "off"
end, "\n"
    end
  end
  def connect(v)
    if @inputs.length >= 1 then
      raise TypeError.new("Too many input connections.")
    end
    super(v)
  end
end


# Base for input devices.  Mostly deals will collecting
connections.
class InputDevice
  def initialize
    @targs = []
  end

  # Add a connection
  def join(g)
    @targs.push(g.connect(false))
  end
```

```ruby
  def joinmany(*p)
    p.each { |i| self.join(i); }
  end


  def outlinks
    return @targs
  end

end


# Switch bank.  Connects to any number of gates, and will feed them a
# binary number (as a string).  Connections start with LSB.  Initially,
# all the switches are off.
class SwitchBank < InputDevice


  # Send a number.  Can take an integer or a string.
  def set(n)
    if n.is_a?(TrueClass) || n.is_a?(FalseClass) then
      @targs.each { | x | x.signal(n) }
    elsif n.is_a?(Integer) then
      @targs.each { | x | x.signal(n&1 == 1); n >>= 1 }
    else
      # Assume n is an ascii string of 1's and 0's.
```

```
    if n.length < @targs.length then
      n = ('o' * (@targs.length - n.length)) + n
    end
    sub = n.length - 1
    @targs.each { | x | x.signal(n[sub].chr != "o"); sub -=
1 }
  end
end


# This is like switch, but it keeps the circuit active
during each
  # sending.
  def value=(n)
    Gate.activate
    self.set(n)
    Gate.deactivate
  end

end

# Send a pulse (clock tick?)
class Pulser < InputDevice

  def pulse
    Gate.activate
```

```ruby
    @targs.each { |t| t.signal(true); }
    @targs.each { |t| t.signal(false); }
    Gate.deactivate
  end
end
```

# Conclusion

Thank you again for downloading this book!

I hope this book was able to help you to learn how to write with the Ruby Programming Language.

The next step is to practice your new found coding skills.

Finally, if you enjoyed this book, please take the time to share your thoughts and post a review on Amazon. It'd be greatly appreciated!

Thank you and good luck!

## Description:

Those who are efficient in the Ruby programming language is very high in demand right now. If you are unsure of how to do this, this book will guide your form step one in a coding project all the way through to the end.

You will learn how to program in no time. Follow along with the book to get the drift on how to use Ruby. After you master Ruby, you can move on to Ruby on Rails, which is the framework that goes with Ruby. You will become a master programmer using the user-friendliest programming language ever developed. Land jobs or even write your own coding for a sweet web application. The sky is the limit once you have read, practiced, and learned the Ruby programming language.

CPSIA information can be obtained
at www.ICGtesting.com
Printed in the USA
LVHW010520200720
660991LV00016B/317